To the wise counselor who guided me into the truth with gentleness and love.

Gentleness: The Pathway to the Heart

ISBN: 979-8-3304-6931-4

English Standard Version Bible. (n.d.). Bible. ESV, DailyVerses.net. Retrieved April 6, 2023, from https://dailyverses.net/

New International Version Bible. (n.d.). Bible. NIV, DailyVerses.net. Retrieved April 6, 2023, from https://dailyverses.net/

New Living Translation Bible. (n.d.). Bible. NLV, DailyVerses.net. Retrieved April 6, 2023, from https://dailyverses.net/

FRUITY JOURNALS

Gentleness

The Pathway to the Heart

from the author

I am delighted that you have accepted the mission to be fruitful and multiply! Fruity Journals is a book series based on cultivating the fruit of God's Spirit in your life. In this journal, I share God inspired wisdom and life experiences that have pushed me closer to Him.

Fruity Journals will help the garden of your heart to flourish with peace, joy, kindness, gentleness, patience, faithfulness, self control, love and goodness. And God's word tells us that out of the abundance of the heart, the mouth speaks. You will witness God's fruit develop in your character, mind, and heart as this book takes you into the caverns of your life and offers you practical prompts for digging and soul searching.

This journal is for women just like you. Women who want to take their relationship deeper with God. Sometimes you have to go down before you can go up! Everyone likes to look at a pretty garden, but the truth is, it is messy. It is a process and every stage is not cute, but the results of health and beauty are to be treasured.

Sometimes, our gardens are nurtured by storms. The next time you go through one of life's storms, you can have the supernatural peace that keeps your mind and heart at ease. This journal series offers you daily tools to brighten your inner light and color your life with the vibrancy of God's goodness.

Okay, that is enough from me. This is the start of your spiritual self care journey.

AMBER JOY THAXTON, LPC

1 Do not rebuke an older
man harshly, but exhort
him as if he were your
father. Treat younger men
as brothers, 2 older women
as mothers, and younger
women as sisters, with
absolute purity. 3 Give
proper recognition to those
widows who are really in
need. 4 But if a widow has
children or grandchildren,
these should learn first
of all to put their religion
into practice by caring for
their own family and so
repaying their parents and
grandparents, for this is
pleasing to God.

1 Timothy 5:1-4 NIV

DAY 1

Treating others as God desires for his sons and daughters can often require some help from the Holy Spirit. If we're honest, our ability to honor others often hinges on our feelings about them or whether we think they "deserve" kindness, respect, or generosity. Yet Paul reminds us in this pastoral letter that we're called to submit our hearts to God's instructions, regardless of these personal judgments.

Please also note that this passage is referring to confrontation. Even when we must face difficult issues, God provides a way to do so by putting our faith into action. We are to treat older men with empathy, as we would a father; younger men as brothers; older women with the respect due a mother; and younger women with the purity of a sister. We are also expected to take special care of the widows in our family because this pleases our father in heaven.

In this, we witness the character of God through His fatherly heart. A good father cares for his children and teaches them to do the same. When others encounter God's sons and daughters, they should recognize them by the fruits of the Spirit within.

Take inventory of the soil of your heart today. What would the way you treat your family say about your fruit?

DATE: / / S M T W T F S

You make your saving help my shield; your help has made me great.

2 Samuel 22:36 NIV

DAY 2

Gentleness is an essential quality for godliness—a quality of the heart.

The Bible references God's gentleness in many ways. Pay attention to how God intervenes with humanity in scripture. The help that comes from God Almighty is His power, which He graciously applies to our lives. Each day, God offers us the choice to invite Him into our lives and situations. He does not beg, force, or bully us into obedience. Now, make no mistake: God is omnipotent, and His will will be done. Yet He lets you choose which side of history you want to stand on. You decide whether you want to be a vessel or a villain to God.

For those of us who choose God, we have experienced how gently He works His way into our hearts. Sharing such fruit with others means learning to channel our power in service to others. We see this meek submission directed to parents, children, husbands, wives, leaders, neighbors, etc. God cares about our relationship with one another. God cares deeply about our relationships. His help shields us from pain and destruction, guiding us toward health and restoration.

Today, let's pray for the spirit of gentleness to flow in our relationships.

Dear God, we see throughout Your word the way You love and liberate Your children. What an honor it is to call the Alpha and Omega both my Lord and my Father. God, I ask for Your help in the positions of power I am in. Help me to approach (person/situation) with gentleness. I want my words to be helpful and restorative. Be glorified in my life.

Amen.

DATE: / / S M T W T F S

6When Jesus saw him
lying there and learned
that he had been in this
condition for a long time,
he asked him, “Do you
want to get well?”
7“Sir,” the invalid replied,
“I have no one to help
me into the pool when
the water is stirred.
While I am trying to get
in, someone else goes
down ahead of me.”
8Then Jesus said to him,
“Get up! Pick up your
mat and walk.”

John 5:6-8 NIV

DAY 3

It's amazing what you can learn about people simply by listening to them. Having counseled for about ten years, I spend most of my days listening to others share their lives. I couldn't imagine a better career! I get to spend time with God's most beautiful creations, each one uniquely made in His image.

I have to credit God for the success I've found in my career. Much of my approach with clients is shaped by the way I've experienced, read, and learned that Jesus connects with us.

Jesus teaches us 3 vital things when it comes to connecting with others.
1.Our encounters with others should liberate them in some way.
2. People are not their problems.
3. Every story is redeemable.

Jesus' approach to people is laced with gentleness and compassion. Gentleness requires that we slow down and pay attention to details. This man was sitting by the pool. I imagine Jesus could have walked past the water and splashed it on everyone that was inflicted with an element and said, "Be healed in my name" and moved on to the next prayer meeting. Instead, he took the time to connect personally with this man. Our all-powerful, all-knowing God, who holds time in His hands, entered our world as a baby—allowing us to see His character in the gentle unfolding of His love, starting with the virgin Mary. Clearly, God is not in a rush. If you're feeling pressured to get healing, find a shortcut to success, or push your relationship to reach the altar, whatever the strain you may be feeling, I want to invite you to give it to Jesus and find rest in knowing that God is gentle and sometimes he has entered into your situation and you just haven't noticed!

What comes to mind when you read today's devotional?
What's something you need God to refresh your perspective about?

DATE: / /　　S M T W T F S

39 Many of the
Samaritans from that
town believed in him
because of the woman's
testimony, "He told me
everything I ever did."
40 So when the
Samaritans came to him,
they urged him to stay
with them, and he stayed
two days. 41 And because
of his words many more
became believers.

John 4:39-41 NIV

DAY 4

Have you ever read the story of the woman at the well?

Here's a quick recap: A Samaritan woman going about her daily routine of drawing water unexpectedly encounters Jesus. Culturally, this was unusual—Jews and Samaritans didn't interact, but thank God, Jesus doesn't let any barrier keep us from His love!

After this epic encounter, the woman returns to her town, and the story continues in John 4:39. Imagine bumping into Jesus in the grocery store aisle by the milk and eggs, where He proceeds to tell you everything about yourself—the good, the bad, and even the hidden secrets. However, He says it in a way that makes you want to stay and hear more. His words are so full of grace and kindness that she wants to introduce Him to her husband, her side boyfriends, friends—anyone who will listen.

Pay close attention, the Bible says; because of his words, many more became believers. How we communicate with others is important. Words can make or break the bond between hearts. Even when addressing something as personal as her past, Jesus speaks with her privately, sparing her any public shame or embarrassment. He opens the conversation by asking her for a drink of water, subtly affirming her worth and what she has to offer. He listens carefully to her responses, free of premeditated answers that might overlook her heart. Through this encounter, Jesus not only reveals the character of a believer but also demonstrates the deep importance of community and unity in God's kingdom.

Take a moment to read Mark 4 and reflect on the character of Christ. What do you notice about the way he connects with others? What are some qualities you appreciate about yourself that enable you to bond with people?

DATE: / / S M T W T F S

1 I love the Lord, for he heard
my voice;
he heard my cry for mercy.

2 Because he turned his ear
to me,
I will call on him as long as
I live.

3 The cords of death
entangled me,
the anguish of the grave
came over me;
I was overcome by
distress and sorrow.

4 Then I called on the name
of the Lord:
"Lord, save me!"

5 The Lord is gracious
and righteous;
our God is full of compassion.

6 The Lord protects
the unwary;
when I was brought low,
he saved me.

Psalm 116:1-6 NIV

DAY 5

Have you ever been in a place of despair? Can you remember a time when life's stresses felt overwhelming and you longed deeply for relief? Psalm 116 feels like it picks up right at the diary entry for that very moment. The tone conveys both the anguish of pain and the liberating hope and healing that come from God's gentle rescue.

God hears your cries; His ears are tuned to your voice. He is a reliable Savior. No problem is too great, no diagnosis too severe, no debt too overwhelming, no heartbreak too deep—there is always hope. We serve a God who knows his way around betrayal, fear, doubt, lack, and slavery. Nothing can separate us from His love. The Lord is gracious and righteous, pouring unearned blessings into the lives of those who believe in Him. The Lord is full of compassion, and he is present to lift your heavy burdens and revive your heavy heart. **You are safe with God.** He brings supernatural rest because He is good.

What do you notice about God's approach to the brokenhearted? Take time to pray for those around you who may be hurting and declare their liberation from pain and sorrow today!

DATE: / /

S M T W T F S

You are safe
with God.

40 Jesus answered him,
"Simon, I have something to
tell you."
"Tell me, teacher," he said.
41 "Two people owed money
to a certain moneylender.
One owed him five hundred
denarii, and the other fifty.
42 Neither of them had the
money to pay him back, so
he forgave the debts of both.
Now which of them will love
him more?"
43 Simon replied, "I suppose
the one who had the bigger
debt forgiven."
"You have judged correctly,"
Jesus said.

Luke 7:40-43 NIV

DAY 6

Jesus' approach to teaching complex moral lessons is remarkable.

He takes challenging topics like prejudice and classism and breaks them down with simple yet powerful examples. As a mother of a seven-year-old firstborn daughter who thinks she knows everything, I can relate to the challenge of communicating effectively with someone who feels she has life all figured out. Don't get me wrong—my daughter is the sweetest girl I know! She genuinely believes she's doing us a favor by sharing her insights, convinced she has the answers to life's mysteries. I have been able to take a lesson out of Jesus' teacher manual by learning how he uses gentle and thoughtful words to bind love and truth together.

1. He respects his 'students' by addressing them by name.
2. He makes sure he has their attention and interest.
3. He shares a parable that is relatable.
4. He checks for understanding.

Whether as a parent, teacher, friend, or neighbor, we often find ourselves needing to communicate with care. Authenticity sometimes requires us to address conflict, and Jesus shows us a wise, gentle approach. Remember, gentleness brings freedom. What do you notice about Jesus' approach with Simon? What can you learn from Jesus to enhance your conflict resolution skills?

DATE: / /   S M T W T F S

15 People were also
bringing babies to Jesus
for him to place his
hands on them. When
the disciples saw this,
they rebuked them.
16 But Jesus called the
children to him and said,
"Let the little children
come to me, and do
not hinder them, for the
kingdom of God belongs
to such as these. 17 Truly
I tell you, anyone who will
not receive the kingdom
of God like a little child
will never enter it."

Luke 18:15-17 NIV

DAY 7

The disciples cherished their time with Jesus and spent each day learning what He valued. They once mistakenly assumed that children weren't significant enough to warrant Jesus' attention, but Jesus quickly corrected them, speaking directly to the children and bringing them close. He then affirmed their worth by explaining how precious they are to him. He did not belittle them; rather, He elevated them and admonished that they be protected, prioritized, and seen as models for true followers of God.

We, too, are God's children, yet many of us feel unworthy of His blessings by midday, disqualifying ourselves in our minds over small mistakes. This passage highlights the vulnerability of children, especially in their early years. What is it about babies that makes them such exemplary heirs? Babies model their behaviors on those around them—they learn to smile, walk, and talk by observing others. From the womb, they faithfully rely on their source for safety, security, and nourishment.

If you've been harsh or overly critical toward yourself lately, remember that you are a child of God. Reference the gentle tone Jesus takes with the vulnerable and practice adapting the tone and the language to how you address yourself. You are precious to God! You are made in His image. Aside from God, you can do nothing. So if you're feeling worn out, pause and take a moment to draw your heart, mind, and soul to the Lord. He is with you at this very moment, reminding you that He loves you just as you are!

DATE: / / S M T W T F S

[13] What you heard from
me, keep as the pattern
of sound teaching, with
faith and love in Christ
Jesus. [14] Guard the
good deposit that was
entrusted to you—guard
it with the help of the
Holy Spirit who lives
in us.

2 Timothy 1:13-14 NIV

DAY 8

How can we bear any fruit of God's Spirit if we don't have a seed deposited in our hearts? Jesus was the seed planted in humanity, changing our lives forever. Christ brought hope and promise. The Holy Spirit in our lives is like the process of photosynthesis, making it possible for the love of Jesus to grow in our hearts and spread from our lives into the world.

We guard the truth of God that frees us because, without the seed of truth, there is no sustainability to our freedom or faith. It doesn't matter how long you've been a believer—whether you came to God at fifteen or fifty-one, we must be intentional about protecting God's gifts by fanning the flame of His gift. Fanning the flame happens when we worship with praise from our lips, clapping of our hands, and dancing of our feet. We have the power to transform an atmosphere from darkness to light just by exalting the Son of God.

To be timid and to be gentle are very different. In 2 Timothy, we are reminded of what we have through the Holy Spirit: power, love, and self-discipline. How essential are these qualities for gentleness? Think of gentleness as being powered by love and best demonstrated through self-discipline.

What good has been deposited in you?
How do you share this wealth?

DATE: / /　　S M T W T F S

But I did not want to do anything without your consent, so that any favor you do would not seem forced but would be voluntary.

Philemon 1:14 NIV

DAY 9

When my oldest child started school, I remember how much she loved her kindergarten teacher. Every day after school, she would cheerfully return home and tell us about her day. She would talk about the songs she sang, the games she played, and the things she learned in her class. It was a special excitement each day. I loved hearing about her day. From time to time, she would accidently call me by her teacher's name. "Mrs. Foster, oops, I mean mom," she would say. Did I think I was being replaced? No, of course not, but I knew she adored her and felt loved by her.

My daughter spent the majority of her day with her teacher. This is the person who would feed her, keep her safe, and make sure she was learning and having fun. And it was because of that special relationship that correction came easy with my daughter. Emery knew that when her teacher addressed an issue with her, it was coming from a place of love because her teacher built a strong bond and relationship with her.

This passage teaches us about the holy submission we are to have to God. God invested in a relationship with us through sending his son Jesus. The Son of God walked with people, prayed with them, fed them, and healed them. Jesus built relationships while on earth through words and deeds. And God, who is sovereign, knows the power of a good teacher. A good teacher does not just love the lessons; a good teacher loves the students to whom the lessons are being taught. The Holy Spirit, also referred to in the passage as the Spirit of Truth, is a gift to believers because it is evidence of God's passion for those He loves to be transformed by truth and rewarded with peace.

Read John 14:15-31 and write out the roles of the Holy Spirit. Next, write about what God is instructing you to do. Consider how you can display holy submission to God's Spirit.

DATE: / /　　S M T W T F S

23 Don’t have anything to
do with foolish and stupid
arguments, because
you know they produce
quarrels. 24 And the Lord’s
servant must not be
quarrelsome but must be
kind to everyone, able to
teach, not resentful.
25 Opponents must be
gently instructed, in the
hope that God will grant
them repentance leading
them to a knowledge of the
truth, 26 and that they will
come to their senses and
escape from the trap of the
devil, who has taken them
captive to do his will.

2 Timothy 2:23-26 NIV

DAY 10

The world grows bolder every day in the lies it believes.

To the world, day is night and night is day. Evil is good, and good is evil. People make up rules and create their own standards to live by. For believers, it can become sad and exhausting to witness the deeds of darkness infect this world. But we cannot let sadness, anger, or pride get the best of us. Do not lose hope in God. He is still the way, the truth, and the life! Be careful not to get drawn into hot-topic debates with those who do not seek truth but rather want to stir up confusion and hatred.

Things like abuse, perversion, and greed are sin issues that start in the heart. The most secret sins require the most love, power, and self-discipline to address. When having heartfelt discussions about heavy topics, always approach them in love. Never allow your personal opinions or feelings to become the driving force. You can stand firm in God's truth while gently reaching out to others. Our job is not to convince. Our responsibility as believers is to lead with love as we share the truth. **Leave room for the Holy Spirit to do the transformational work** that only love and truth can accomplish at God's appointed time.

On a scale of 1-10, what does your gentleness meter stand at when confronted with sin? Does the way you approach your own sin differ from how you address others'?

Leave room for the Holy Spirit to do the transformational work.

DATE: / /　　S M T W T F S

the

to the

athway
heart

1 Every high priest is
selected from among
the people and is
appointed to represent
the people in matters
related to God, to offer
gifts and sacrifices for
sins. 2 He is able to deal
gently with those who
are ignorant and are
going astray, since he
himself is subject to
weakness.

Hebrews 5:1-2 NLT

DAY 11

Have you ever felt weighed down by guilt? Ever allowed yourself to do something that left you feeling soaked by the wet blanket of shame?

I remember in my youth when I compromised my boundaries while dating. I felt so ashamed of myself. I isolated myself from everyone and became a victim of fear. I remember how two little words shattered my glass house. Having a loved one hear my story and utter the sobering words, "Me too," rocked my world—or more accurately, it rocked the prison walls that sin and shame tried to keep me bound by.

Though we serve a God who never sinned, He sent His Son Jesus, who was subjected to the same pain, darkness, and temptations that we face—and more. You can boldly approach God's throne because He knows the breaking point of your strength. We represent Christ when, like the high priest, we can be self-aware enough to share our vulnerabilities with others and offer them gentle words of encouragement that restore.

What part of your story have you been vulnerable enough to share with others? How did you witness God use what the enemy meant for evil and turn it around for your good?

DATE: / / S M T W T F S

4 Rejoice in the Lord
always. I will say it
again: Rejoice! 5 Let your
gentleness be evident
to all. The Lord is near.

Philippians 4:4-5 NIV

DAY 12

There is power in numbers. Whether it's the result of the donuts you eat or the dollars you deposit into a bank account, it will amount to something in time! This truth applies to our words too. What you say again and again has tremendous effect. If you find yourself constantly saying, "I'm tired" or "I am so mad" or "I'm broke"—whatever it may be—your feet will begin to follow what your heart believes. When we rejoice in the Lord again and again, we usher more of God's blessings into our lives simply because we are elevating our mindset to see from the vantage point of faith.

Gentleness is the pathway to the heart that leads to liberation. There is nothing like exalting the name of Jesus. There is power in His name, and worship puts you in the presence of the One who raises the dead, walks on water, opens the sea, and sits on the throne of all power and authority.

Your gentleness cannot help but be evident when you turn your heart toward heaven and your voice echoes the angels in praise to the King. I encourage you to slow down today. Don't speed through your daily reading or check off another task on your to-do list without taking a moment to offer up praises to the King.

In your journal today, write what you are rejoicing about.

DATE: / /   S M T W T F S

8 The Lord is good and
does what is right;
he shows the proper path
to those who go astray.

9 He leads the humble in
doing right, teaching
them his way.

10 The Lord leads with
unfailing love and
faithfulness all who
keep his covenant and
obey his demands.

Psalms 25:8-10 NLT

DAY 13

Gentleness is recognized by both its actions and intentions.

We recently added a new family member to our crew at Christmas—a two-year-old Goldendoodle. Though this little guy can be so cute and cuddly at times, he doesn't have a gentle bone in his body. When he wants you to pet him, he'll get your hand on his body by any means necessary. He'll use his nose to slide under your hand and then quickly nod his head up to position your hand on his head for a pat. If anyone in the family is hugging or in a prayer circle, he'll pounce like a mosquito on a summer night, but thank God that He isn't like a clumsy 75-pound puppy who doesn't know his strength.

God is all-knowing, all-powerful, and always present. The Lord touches our lives intending to bring us closer to Himself by way of love. God is good, and He is an excellent teacher. Whether you're a scholar or can't get by without a tutor, God is a good teacher, and His ways are both gentle and relentless.

Considering the type of student you are, what qualities of good teachers have helped you succeed over your lifetime?

DATE: / / S M T W T F S

[11] "Go out and stand before
me on the mountain," the
Lord told him. And as Elijah
stood there, the Lord passed
by, and a mighty windstorm
hit the mountain. It was
such a terrible blast that the
rocks were torn loose, but
the Lord was not in the wind.
After the wind there was an
earthquake, but the Lord was
not in the earthquake. [12] And
after the earthquake there
was a fire, but the Lord was
not in the fire. And after the
fire there was the sound of a
gentle whisper. [13] When Elijah
heard it, he wrapped his face
in his cloak and went out and
stood at the entrance of
the cave.

1 Kings 19:11-13 NIV

DAY 14

There is nothing like God's voice cutting through chaos. Over the rumbling rocks, the howl of the wind, the vibrations of the ground beneath his feet, and the white noise of fire, nothing could arrest Elijah's attention like the gentle voice of God Almighty.

There are certain things in the Bible that I'm so glad God didn't choose me to go through. Honestly, I think if there were ever a book called "Bible Bloopers," my name would likely make its debut. However, in all seriousness, this also brings to mind how sometimes chaos looks different for each of us. It might sound like constant arguments with your children or the obnoxious silent treatment from your spouse. It might sound like the buzzer that beeps when your card is declined in the checkout line or the piercing cries of a colicky baby. It might sound like the cry of a nation under siege. Many things can try to grab our attention and keep us paralyzed with fear or pain. God doesn't compete by yelling over the happenings in our lives; His gentle voice moves past our eyes and directly into our hearts.

God has a way of getting our attention, and He never uses the evil devices of this world. God is holy, and He doesn't look, sound, or act anything like the prince of darkness or the demonic forces that govern this world. Sometimes, when we're going through difficult times, we struggle to hear God. I want to upgrade your faith today: know that nothing will keep you from God's love. He is always at work. He is His Word, and His Word brings life. Sometimes when we think we can't hear God, it's because we've already heard Him, and we need to accept the truth and stop ignoring it.

What is something that you know God has said? How can you take this truth and use it to encourage yourself or others?

DATE: / / S M T W T F S

[5] For those who live
according to the flesh
set their minds on the
things of the flesh, but
those who live according
to the Spirit set their
minds on the things of
the Spirit. [6] For to set
the mind on the flesh
is death, but to set the
mind on the Spirit is
life and peace. [7] For the
mind that is set on the
flesh is hostile to God,
for it does not submit to
God's law; indeed,
it cannot.

Romans 8:5-7 ESV

DAY 15

Have you ever tried to learn something new while feeling stressed or overwhelmed? There's a reason classroom management is a vital skill for grade school teachers. An effective educator uses their environment to the advantage of students by considering how lighting, sound, and even the décor and material on the walls will either pose barriers or be conducive to student attention, enhancing the chances of the information being absorbed.

We all have a built-in stress response commonly referred to as "fight, flight, or freeze" that helps our senses become hyper-focused on our external environment. This defense mechanism helps us zero in on threats and escape or overcome danger. You may be wondering if you picked up your devotional today or your psychology book by accident. Remember—God made psychology, and He set the standard for good teachers!

The Lord is drawing you close. He has released you from the weight of your stress and is inviting you to find rest in the safety of His presence. He offers us a yoke to keep us connected with Him because He knows we learn best by example and repetition. Don't worry about trying to ace God's class. **You will always be loved 100%.**

Is there anything causing you stress today? There is no burden God cannot handle. What is causing you to feel weighed down or distracted? Make a list on the next page, and with every stroke of your pen, imagine you are leaving the words on this page and every care is being transferred to God.

DATE: / /

S M T W T F S

You will **always** be loved 100%

[1] As they approached
Jerusalem and came to
Bethphage on the Mount
of Olives, Jesus sent two
disciples, [2] saying to them,
"Go to the village ahead of
you, and at once you will find
a donkey tied there, with her
colt by her. Untie them and
bring them to me. [3] If anyone
says anything to you, say
that the Lord needs them,
and he will send them right
away."

[4] This took place to fulfill
what was spoken through
the prophet:

[5] "Say to Daughter Zion,
'See, your king comes to
you, gentle and riding on
a donkey, and on a colt,
the foal of a donkey.'"

Matthew 21:1-5 NIV

DAY 16

Prophecy is a unique gift from God. I remember being in my late 20s when I found myself struggling to adapt to being a first-time mom. Most days I felt like I was doing everything wrong, and it seemed almost everything would make her cry. One evening, some girlfriends of mine were getting together, so I packed up my daughter and we headed across town. We weren't even there an hour before we found ourselves worshiping God and praying. It was beautiful. There was a woman in the group who had the gift of prophecy, and she began sharing different words with each of us. When she got to me, she said, "When your daughter turns 2, she will have a brother." Everyone else had received words about becoming successful and traveling the world, so you can understand how this felt out of left field.

We were living in Tulsa, Oklahoma, when I noticed I wasn't feeling well one evening. We began to consider what could be causing me to feel hot, clammy, and tired. So we grabbed a pregnancy test to rule out the possibility. I remember Trey, my daughter, and I standing in the bathroom staring at the pregnancy test as we waited for the signal to tell us yay or nay. As you can guess, the rest was history. My daughter Emery turned 2 a month later, and I was pregnant! We knew this was the son that had been prophesied about.

I tell you this story because prophecy is essential to our faith. When God finds it necessary to tip us off to what is to come, often it's because He wants us to know that He is at work even when we cannot see it. The prophecy of our gentle Savior was spoken prior to Jesus's birth. When Jesus began His ministry, the political climate was tense; there was racial tension, hypocrisy, and false gods being worshiped, but God had a plan all along.

Read Zechariah 9:9 and Matthew 21:1–5.

There is a 400-year gap between when the Old Testament and New Testament were written. Why do you think God intended for us to have this information prior to His Son's coming? How does this impact your faith and understanding of God?

DATE: / / S M T W T F S

1 By the humility and
gentleness of Christ, I
appeal to you—I, Paul, who
am "timid" when face to face
with you, but "bold" toward
you when away! 2 I beg you
that when I come I may not
have to be as bold as I expect
to be toward some people
who think that we live by the
standards of this world. 3 For
though we live in the world,
we do not wage war as the
world does. 4 The weapons
we fight with are not the
weapons of the world. On
the contrary, they have
divine power to demolish
strongholds.

2 Corinthians 10:1-4 NIV

DAY 17

Notice how brother Paul is setting the record straight. He is announcing that he is ministering out of the power of God, not his own flesh. You can recognize a tree by its fruit. The qualities of God are humble and gentle, but the counterfeit of our flesh is timidity. Paul admits that his nature is to be timid, which means weak and lacking confidence, but gentleness and humility are rooted in power, meanwhile submitted to the authority of the will of God to establish his purpose.

May this give you hope today. No matter your shortcomings, when you surrender your life to God, he will endow you with his Spirit, which will produce undeniable fruit. As a believer, it is good to know what you were like before you knew the Lord, so that you can recognize the undeniable difference God's love brings into our lives. The power of God reforms us. It makes us new creatures and positions us as righteous. We cannot do this on our own.

Do not allow yourself to remain intimidated by your weakness; you can do all things through Christ, who strengthens you. As you journal today, I want you to write a list of your qualities before you came into an intimate relationship with Christ. And then I want you to take a moment to pray and ask God to bring to the surface who he says you are and the qualities that you have in Christ Jesus.

DATE: / /

S M T W T F S

But the wisdom from above is first of all pure. It is also peace loving, **gentle** at all times, and willing to yield to others. It is full of mercy and the fruit of good deeds. It shows no favoritism and is always sincere.

James 3:17 NLT

DAY 18

Everywhere we look, there is a flood of information and advice round the clock. On the commute from home to work, there are billboards and radio advertisements. Our devices curate ads to draw us in based on our interests. Advice is everywhere: social media, friends, television, but James warns us not just to take advice from any old place but to consider the source of the places we receive information.

He says to consider who is wise. Wisdom is knowledge that is applied. Often we are so quick to listen to the loudest voices in society, those with the most followers, or the rich and famous, but God does not share the same standards as the world. Those we glean from should be humble, live good lives, and display their wisdom through words and actions. Bitterness and self-interest are poisonous and can infect work, friendships, and marriages, so we must guard our hearts from following the advice of anyone and everyone.

Do not just open your heart to anyone, but measure the source of your advice by the godly wisdom qualities—peaceful, loving, considerate, submissive, full of mercy—and produce good fruit that is genuine. These are peacemakers, and the seeds they sow are righteous.

Your heart is good soil, so be careful what is planted there because it will produce a harvest. List 5 people or sources of advice that have the privilege to speak into your life. What qualifies them?

DATE: / /　　S M T W T F S

Now when Jesus saw the crowds,
He went up on the mountain; and
after He sat down, His disciples
came to Him. 2 And He opened
His mouth and began to teach
them, saying,

3 "Blessed are the poor in spirit,
for theirs is the kingdom of
heaven.
4 "Blessed are those who mourn,
for they will be comforted.
5 "Blessed are the **gentle,** for they
will inherit the earth.
6 "Blessed are those who hunger
and thirst for righteousness,
for they will be satisfied.
7 "Blessed are the merciful, for
they will receive mercy.
8 "Blessed are the pure in heart,
for they will see God.
9 "Blessed are the peacemakers,
for they will be called sons of
God.
10 "Blessed are those who have
been persecuted for the sake
of righteousness, for theirs is
the kingdom of heaven.

Matthew 5:1-10 NASB

DAY 19

This is one of the most well-known sermons of Jesus that was delivered on a mountainside. The Sermon on the Mount was taught to the disciples that were drawing near to Jesus. How wonderful it must have been in the number of those who got to sit at his feet and be taught the principles of the kingdom. Something I think most of us can agree on as children of God is that the ways of our father are not our ways. Our faith is not guided by common sense but by the will and heart of God.

The 8 Beatitudes are more than a make-lemons-out-of-lemonade message. This is a message from a God who walks with his people and sees their hurt, their painful circumstances, but more importantly, their hearts. Jesus realigned our hope with God and not the good or the bad that is happening around us. Christ was sent to elevate our eyes and to set our hopes on things that are outside of this world. God wants to take you further than where your feet can take you. God wants to take you deeper than your own knowledge and wisdom can take you.

God has supreme blessings for you, whether you can see it or not. Sometimes circumstances can be so hard that our thoughts can get stuck dwelling on the misery. What we focus on becomes magnified, and like an infection, it produces heavy feelings, then it creeps into causing distortions in our thoughts, and eventually it grows into our lifestyle. Cut the issue off at the root by keeping the reminder of your supreme blessing around your finger. Do not lose sight of the promise of God. Write them on your bathroom mirror, place a sticky note in your car, at your desk at work, and jot it down on your hand. Highlight the beatitude that you need to hang on to today and write it 5x in your journal. Commit it to memory and meditate on seeing God's word come to life.

DATE: / / S M T W T F S

15 but sanctify Christ
as Lord in your hearts,
always being ready
to make a defense to
everyone who asks you
to give an account for
the hope that is in you,
yet with **gentleness** and
reverence; 16 and keep
a good conscience so
that in the thing in which
you are slandered, those
who revile your good
behavior in Christ will be
put to shame.

1 Peter 3:15-16 NASB

DAY 20

The call to testify about the goodness of our Lord and Savior can feel like a daunting task for many. When we think about sharing how we came to know Jesus or grow in our faith, it can seem overwhelming—and for good reason. Our story with God has neither beginning nor end. Scripture tells us that God knew us before we were in our mother's womb, yet most of us don't even remember our life before age three. It's challenging to tell a story when we're uncertain of its beginning, but what we can share is our personal journey of faith.

The work of Jesus Christ on the cross saved us, and it's the presence of God's Spirit that empowers us to live each day as conquerors. I grew up in a Christian household and cannot remember a time when God wasn't part of my life. What stands out clearly, however, is the ongoing challenge to keep God first and the consequences of allowing other things to occupy the throne of my heart.

Recently, my husband went out of town for three nights and four days—the longest I'd ever been alone with our two children. Within 24 hours, I felt overwhelmed managing everyone's schedules: school drop-offs, football games, playdates, and homework, not to mention preparing dinner, giving baths, and handling toddler moodiness. I was about due for a meltdown myself. Then, just hours before my husband's return on Friday night, my daughter became ill and threw up all over herself.

The testimony here is that in my exhaustion and stress, when that final challenge came, I was providentially at the home of some friends from church. During our first visit to their beautiful house, this family's response to my daughter's situation touched my heart deeply. I witnessed God's love firsthand through this husband and wife who, without hesitation, provided towels and clean clothes with genuine kindness. They showed no concern about their white carpet or their living room floor. I thank God this happened while we were surrounded by His people—the evening would have been far different had I been alone at home. God's love shone brilliantly through their gentleness and compassion. Life presents its challenges, but God's love prevails every time.

(See next page for journal exercise.)

DATE: / / S M T W T F S

It's testimony time...

1. When was a time you felt far from God?

2. How did you see God come to your rescue?

3. How has your encounter with God impacted you?

12 Therefore, as God's
chosen people, holy
and dearly loved,
clothe yourselves with
compassion, kindness,
humility, **gentleness**
and patience. 13 Bear
with each other and
forgive one another
if any of you has a
grievance against
someone. Forgive as the
Lord forgave you. 14 And
over all these virtues
put on love, which binds
them all together in
perfect unity.

Colossians 3:12-14 NIV

DAY 21

When you live the life of a believer, you soon realize that there is no one-stop shop for becoming a perfect Christian. In fact, there is no perfect Christian; we are children of God who are being raised by our father in heaven in the righteousness of Christ. Part of growing up means you change over time. The way you walk changes, your communication develops, and you begin to be more active and accomplish new things. Even the way you dress changes. Here we see that as we mature in Christ, we put to death what belongs to our former nature. Paul references in verse 5 sexual immorality, lust, evil desires, and greed, which stir up the wrath of God.

As God's children, we should aim to please our father and to put on the new garments he has provided for us in our new life. Garments that are more fitting for who we are, garments that make you and those around you feel appreciated, valued, and honored. There is nothing like putting on a new outfit that accentuates all your best qualities. Also, be sure to top this outfit off with the staple item that will bring it all together: love. Love binds all of our godly qualities to the source, which is God. Our job is to wear the garments and ask the Holy Spirit to help us keep wearing them appropriately. And in the case of godly pursuits, the garments do not get tailored; we do. Invite the Holy Spirit daily to help you get in shape so that when you step out of bed, you look stunning because you are shining from within.

Read Colossians 3:1-14. What are the old garments that no longer fit in your wardrobe? Which garments do you display the best? Take time to reflect on how far you have come in your walk with Christ.

DATE: / / S M T W T F S

2 Be completely humble
and **gentle;** be patient,
bearing with one
another in love. 3 Make
every effort to keep
the unity of the Spirit
through the bond of
peace. 4 There is one
body and one Spirit,
just as you were called
to one hope when you
were called; 5 one Lord,
one faith, one baptism;
6 one God and Father of
all, who is over all and
through all and in all.

Ephesians 4:2-6 NIV

DAY 22

The instructions here are pretty explicit. Be completely humble, gentle, patient, and loving. If I am completely honest, I would rather say, Be confident, assertive, and a little humble and gentle at times. You can sprinkle some love on everything you do, but I do not get to twist what God says to fit my preference anymore than you do. Community, connection, and relationships matter so much to God. As I have been inspired by the Holy Spirit to write on the fruit of the Spirit, I have learned more and more about how farming the things of God is for the gathering of his people to eat and be merry.

God loves us, and he displays much of his care through the actions of those who love him and are called according to his purpose. God does not want for us to be abused, manipulated, or belittled. He instructs us on how to behave and treat each other with the utmost respect because that is how we deserve to be addressed. I know "deserve" is a tough word for "humble" followers of Christ, but here is the thing: do not let your humility be based on false pretenses. If God says you are righteous, why do many of us keep calling ourselves sinners (2 Corinthians 5:21)? If God tells us that you are complete in him, why do many of us say we are not good enough (James 3:2, Colossians 2:10)?

To live a life worthy of the calling of God, you have to first accept that role. If you have accepted that you are a child of God, it is time to raise the standards on all levels. Raise the standard for how you treat others. And raise the standard for how you see yourself. Raise the standard for what you will accept in your relationships. Those who love you should show it in their gentleness, compassion, and patience.

DATE: / /   S M T W T F S

[11] But you, man of God,
flee from all this, and
pursue righteousness,
godliness, faith,
love, endurance and
gentleness. [12] Fight the
good fight of the faith.
Take hold of the eternal
life to which you were
called when you made
your good confession in
the presence of many
witnesses.

1 Timothy 6:11-12 NIV

DAY 23

In the fall of 2010, I packed up my things and left the place I'd called home for the past 16 years, heading to the middle of the country—Tulsa, Oklahoma.

I left my hometown to pursue higher education, and my college years proved formative for many reasons. My character was shaped by both triumphs and trials during this time, and those years are a big part of why I am the woman I am today. College often requires moving to a new place to fully immerse yourself in learning. It's a shift from the familiar school schedule—going from classes to homework to evening play—to a life where studying takes priority, demanding time and dedication. Being around others moving in the same direction provides a synergy that promotes growth and success. Our faith journey is similar: we are called to pursue a higher way of living. Like my 19-year-old self leaving what was familiar, godliness calls us to step beyond our comfort zones.

Pursuing righteousness means seeking to be in right standing with God. It requires studying what it means to be godly, learning to fully accept God's love, and offering it freely to others. It's about walking by faith, learning to sidestep the traps of fear, greed, and pride that would otherwise trip us up.

You were made for this. I believe God is reminding you today that He has called you to a higher purpose. Let this be an invitation to take the pressure off of perfection and to keep pursuing godliness through time spent with God, studying His Word, prayer, and fellowship. Fruit is meant to be shared—so fight the urge to isolate yourself and trust that God is leading you into godly, life-giving relationships.

DATE: / / S M T W T F S

Brethren, even if anyone is caught in any trespass, you who are spiritual, restore such a one in a spirit of **gentleness;** each one looking to yourself, so that you too will not be tempted.

Galatians 6:1 NASB

DAY 24

Are you a trustworthy friend? Can others come to you with their mistakes and missteps and trust that they will not be judged or rejected? Many people have been scared by being vulnerable with people who call themselves Christians just to be labeled and pushed away. To be a safe place for others really starts with self-awareness. Remember that we did not earn our righteousness; we were given forgiveness and love freely by Christ. Christ restored us, and we have the privilege of walking with others and doing the same. Jesus left us his spirit and the mission to make disciples.

According to Jesus, making disciples was a process where they spent time together and had intimate discussions. Jesus validated, encouraged, and forgave them. To be a disciple is to be a child of God, and acceptance in this family is an honor. We are not gatekeepers for the kingdom. We are in the family business of restoration. Restoration starts with the humility of self-awareness. Examine your heart and its motives. Use wisdom when having difficult discussions, and always precede them with prayer.

Here are 3 things to consider when helping to restore others:

1. Jesus' life was given so that we all could have new life.
2. The Holy Spirit does the transformative work that takes place in the heart of man.
3. Gentleness is the pathway to the heart that leads to liberation, not condemnation.

DATE: / / S M T W T F S

“I am sending you out like sheep among wolves. Therefore be as shrewd as snakes and as innocent as doves.

Matthew 10:16 NIV

DAY 25

Opportunity often follows assignments.

If you start your reading a few lines back at Matthew 10, you will notice that each disciple was given a choice to follow Jesus. As they walked with him and learned about the Kingdom of God, they were given the opportunity to leave their old lives behind and start a new journey built on faith in Jesus, the Son of God. At the appointed time, Jesus granted the disciples the authority and power to drive out demons and heal the sick, but this authority was not just for show. We pick up in Matthew 10:16 when Jesus further instructs his disciples to sharpen their skill set. He teaches them the power of being versatile and multidimensional. I do not know where the stigma of simple churchgoers came from; those who follow Jesus are taught to be sharp, keen, and wise in their dealings. Christ also instructs us to remain new creatures who have been forgiven and given back their innocence.

Taking on the gentle nature of a dove and the keen nature of a snake is a roundhouse kick to the throat of the enemy. Our gentle nature opens up doors that give access to the power of God to light up the darkness. God really does equip those he calls! Life is a journey; keep walking with God and keep training yourself in the word. Daily time with God is like laying on the wheel of the potter. God will continue to transform you into his masterpiece.

What do you see when you look at yourself? A mess or a masterpiece? Most of us would say somewhere in between, depending on the day. I believe God is strengthening your confidence to know and believe that he has called you and equipped you for such a time as this.

Opportunity often follows assignments.

DATE: / /　　S M T W T F S

[5] For we never came
with words of flattery,
as you know, nor with a
pretext for greed—God
is witness. [6] Nor did we
seek glory from people,
whether from you or
from others, though
we could have made
demands as apostles
of Christ. [7] But we were
gentle among you, like
a nursing mother taking
care of her own children.

1 Thessalonians 2:5-7 ESV

DAY 26

The gospel means "good news," and it has been entrusted to us. When I was about 16, my mother gave me some of her jewelry—gold earrings with diamonds. This was her way of sharing something special, trusting me to care for it. It was valuable and beautiful. But how much more valuable is the truth that has the power to set everyone free? People will go to great lengths to obtain things of value. Unfortunately, from biblical times to today, some who claim to know God don't share His agenda of love and righteousness.

We need to be cautious about being drawn in by those who associate themselves with the gospel but use decoys to gain trust. Paul warns us to discern between genuine love and insincere praise, reminding us that the motive behind the gospel matters. The gospel doesn't need flashiness or glamor; all that is for people. The gospel is simple—it's good news to those who are lost. If you were stranded on a deserted island, on the brink of despair, gold and money would be meaningless to you. You know what would matter? A savior who comes to rescue you, offering the bread of life and living water. Teachers and representatives of the gospel should display the fruit of God's Spirit. Their approach should be genuine and gentle. Encounters with believers should leave you feeling empowered.

Has there been someone in your life who represented God well? What was it about this person that drew you to them?

DATE: / / S M T W T F S

[1] Remind the people
to be subject to rulers
and authorities, to be
obedient, to be ready
to do whatever is good,
[2] to slander no one,
to be peaceable and
considerate, and always
to be **gentle** toward
everyone.

Titus 3:1-2 NIV

DAY 27

It's easy to be kind to people you like or admire. I love giving gifts and words of affirmation to those who share my values and interests. However, being kind only to those we admire isn't enough; we are called to be peaceable and considerate of ALL men. I love how God leaves no stone unturned, making it clear that He expects us to be at peace with everyone—neighbors, mothers-in-law, politicians, those who love us, and even those who couldn't care less about us.

This scripture begins with "remind them," because sometimes we need a reminder to do hard things. I never have to remind my kids about dessert, but eating vegetables is a constant discussion in our household! Let's be honest—politics and government can be challenging. We must be prayerful and wise when dealing with people of faith and those who aren't. We can't legislate morality, but we are called to take our light into dark places so that it shines, to be ready with good deeds, to usher peace into situations with gentleness and consideration, which sometimes takes prayer and fasting. We can stand for what we believe in without stepping on others.

If you find your buttons are easily pushed by certain people, consider what may lie at the root of the trigger. Is it fear, pain, anger, or unforgiveness? Whatever it is, and whomever it involves, let's bring it to the altar today. Blessings and curses can't flow from the same vessel, so let's invite the Holy Spirit to continue His sanctifying work, counseling us on the buried issues that God wants to free us from.

DATE: / / S M T W T F S

76 And you, child, will be
called the prophet of
the Most High;
for you will go before
the Lord to prepare
his ways,
77 to give knowledge
of salvation
to his people
in the forgiveness
of their sins,
78 because of the
tender mercy of
our God,
whereby the sunrise
shall visit us from
on high

Luke 1:76-78 NIV

DAY 28

These powerful words came from the mouth of Zechariah, the husband of Elizabeth. Elizabeth was unable to conceive, and both she and her husband were elderly and childless. Yet, their circumstances were no obstacle for God. An angel appeared to them with instructions about their unborn son, and even revealed his name. Zechariah, amazed and doubtful, questioned the promise and, as a result, became mute until the baby was born. His voice only returned when he wrote the name given by God—John—on a tablet at the time of his son's birth. This child would grow up to be John the Baptist.

God had a gentle way of reaching Zechariah's heart. Over the nine months of Elizabeth's pregnancy, Zechariah had ample time for reflection. One powerful lesson from this story is not to view our circumstances as too difficult or insignificant for the Lord. Our challenges are opportunities for God's will to unfold, and our words hold power—they can either nurture or negate our faith. In His kindness, God protected Zechariah from his own doubts by giving him a season of silence, allowing him to listen more deeply than he spoke. During this time, Zechariah likely faced the challenge of communicating with others in new ways, but he also grew in observing the presence and fulfillment of God's word right before him. I assume he learned to distinguish between the infallible truth of God's word and his own limited perspective, growing less doubtful and more daring in his faith.

Read Luke 1:26–80 for the full story. What stands out to you when you read it? What do you notice about God and about human nature? How does this impact your life?

DATE: / /　　S M T W T F S

1 A **gentle** answer turns away wrath,
But a harsh word stirs up anger.

Proverbs 15:1 NIV

DAY 29

Have you ever lost your cool, snapped, or "gave someone the business," only to find that it made things worse? I'm not talking about a playful jab like a "yo momma" joke among friends. I mean the kind of anger that builds over time, heating up on the stove of confrontation until it boils over, burning everyone in its path—including you. I call these "lava moments." Our harsh words may feel like a release at the time, but the satisfaction of standing over others never lasts.

Gentle words, on the other hand, come from a calm heart. The word "confrontation" itself implies facing something directly. We should first confront what's going on inside us before addressing outside problems. Learn to recognize when you're feeling hurt, afraid, or offended. These are signals to take a step back, process what you're experiencing, and understand the buildup behind the moment. Always bring your struggles to God before bringing them to others. This way, you'll better understand the true root of the issues and know which ones need to be addressed. A gentle approach can ease even difficult discussions.

Remember, gentleness is a form of communication. While it may not solve every problem instantly, it sets you on the right path.

DATE: / / S M T W T F S

31 For who is God, but the
LORD?
And who is a rock, except
our God?—
32 the God who equipped me
with strength
and made my way
blameless.
33 He made my feet like the
feet of a deer
and set me secure on the
heights.
34 He trains my hands for
war, so that my arms can
bend a bow of bronze.
35 You have given me the
shield of your salvation.
and your right hand
supported me,
and your **gentleness**
made me great.

Psalm 18:31-35 ESV

DAY 30

Our God is a good God! This passage reads like a proud banner of the good news. God's ways reveal His character, and His reputation precedes Him. He doesn't just do everything for us; He shows us time and again that we are made in His image. He doesn't enable our weaknesses—He strengthens and trains us. God allows us to encounter situations that require us to depend on the Spirit within us, the same Spirit through whom we live, move, and have our being. The Lord equips, disciplines, and trains us, and in due season, He stands with us in battle so we can experience His strength through us.

I'm speaking to the mom who feels drained after responding to the endless demands of her family, to the leader with their hands full and mind occupied, and to anyone who feels weary and struggling to hold onto hope. In our weakness, God's strength is made perfect. When you reach this point, the best thing you can do is acknowledge it and confess your need for God. Like a loving parent, He doesn't snatch things from our hands; He lets us see what we're capable of, and when we need Him, He's only a whisper away.

Recite this confession with me today:

God, you are one of a kind. You are my rock, and you have armed me with strength and endurance. You patiently teach and train me to be victorious in all things. Salvation is my shield, and your right hand sustains me. Your gentle nature has penetrated my heart and empowered me to overcome. Amen.

You've made it to the end of the 30-Day Fruity Journal.
It was a pleasure to walk with you through one of God's unique qualities. I hope you enjoyed spending time in the Garden with me.
Remember: You are blessed—now go and be fruitful!

DATE: / / S M T W T F S

My heart is good soil.

Each day with the
help of the Holy Spirit,
I survey my heart.

I believe when I confess
my sins, I am forgiven.

I believe when I cast
my cares, I am free.

Day after day, God
replenishes me from
His well of living water.

And as a result, my
life is blossoming
with Godly fruit.

Amen.

NOTES

www.ingramcontent.com/pod-product-compliance
Ingram Content Group UK Ltd.
Pitfield, Milton Keynes, MK11 3LW, UK
UKHW060404300726
14090UKWH00006B/421

* 9 7 9 8 2 1 8 5 4 7 6 9 1 *